HABITATS
Northern Forests

Robert Snedden

FRANKLIN WATTS
LONDON • SYDNEY

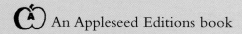 An Appleseed Editions book

First published in 2004 by Franklin Watts
96 Leonard Street, London, EC2A 4XD

Franklin Watts Australia
45–51 Huntley Street, Alexandria, NSW 2015

© 2004 Appleseed Editions

Created by Appleseed Editions Ltd,
Well House, Friars Hill, Guestling, East Sussex, TN35 4ET

Designed by Helen James

ISBN 0 7496 5715 4

A CIP catalogue for this book is available from the British Library.

Photographs by Corbis (Niall Benvie, Tom Brakefield, Nigel J. Dennis; Gallo Images,
Douglas Faulkner, Natalie Fobes, Raymond Gehman, Gunter Marx Photography,
Richard Hamilton Smith, Wolfgang Kaehler, Charles Krebs, Danny Lehman,
George D. Lepp, Joe McDonald, D. Robert & Lorri Franz, Bill Ross, Galen Rowell,
L. Rue, Ron Sanford, Phil Schermeister, Tim Thompson, Jeff Vanuga, Jim Zuckerman,
Tim Zurowski)

Printed and bound in the USA

Contents

Forests of the north wind

The place where a living thing makes its home is called its **habitat**. A habitat can be as small as a damp place under a rotting log, or as big as the ocean. The biggest habitats, such as deserts, forests and mountains, are called **biomes**.

Great evergreen forests

South of the **Arctic Circle**, great forests of evergreen trees spread in an almost unbroken band around the world. Stretching across vast areas of North America, northern Europe and Asia, the northern forest is the world's biggest biome. It accounts for a third of the world's forest area. The forest is like a green crown around the head of the world. Unlike multilayered rainforests, northern (or boreal) forests have only one, uneven layer of trees reaching about 20 metres high. There may be a layer of shrubs growing beneath the big trees. The damp floor of the forest can be thick with mosses and lichens, which also grow on tree trunks and branches.

Boreal forests ring the world like a green crown.

NORTHERN FORESTS / TAIGA

Tall evergreen trees dominate the world's largest biome: the northern forest.

The cold north

Large stretches of **taiga** lie inside the Arctic Circle. The **climate** of the taiga is similar to the **tundra** climate to the north. In fact, it can be colder in the forest in the winter than it is on the tundra. The coldest place in the northern hemisphere during the winter is the forest of eastern Siberia. The main difference between the tundra and the forest is the longer and warmer summer growing season in the forest. To the north, the trees grow smaller until the boreal forest fades into the treeless plains of the tundra.

To the south, evergreen boreal forest gradually gives way to the **deciduous** forests and grasslands of warmer climates.

WHAT'S IN A NAME?

Taiga is the Russian word (meaning land of little sticks) for the northern forests. The word is also used in North America and Europe. The northern forest biome is also called the boreal forest, a name that comes from Boreas, the Greek god of the north wind.

Taiga climate

The climate of the taiga is generally cold, with little rainfall and a short growing season. Frost can blanket the ground for up to ten months of the year in some places.

The climate in the taiga is dominated by the wind that brings bitterly cold air south from the Arctic. The air is dry, too. This is because cold air carries less moisture than warm air. Winter in the taiga stretches over a bleak six or seven months, during which the average temperature stays below freezing. It is dark, cold and snowy, with very long nights. Inside the Arctic Circle there are winter days when the sun does not rise at all. Summer in the taiga is warm, with long days that can last up to 20 hours – even longer inside the Arctic Circle. Although the summer is longer than in the tundra to the north, it is short-lived.

 Boreal forests are the coldest places trees can grow. Further north are the treeless plains of the tundra.

The taiga of Siberia is a typical boreal region.

The watery forest

Much of the taiga is permanently waterlogged and swampy because underground **permafrost** prevents the water from draining away. There is a lot of water in the forest in the form of rivers, streams, lakes, ponds and boggy ground. However, the region doesn't receive much rain. So where does all the water come from?

Most of the lakes of the boreal forest were carved out by **glaciers** during the last **ice age**. The water, the result of melting ice, is very cold. Bogs also form in the holes created by retreating glaciers. The taiga is generally damp because the forest lands are flat. Water doesn't run off easily. The cold climate also plays a part, as water doesn't **evaporate** readily into cold air.

HIGHS AND LOWS

The average winter low temperature in the taiga is -54° Celsius and it can fall below -60° Celsius. The average summer high temperature is 21° Celsius and can reach as high as 40° Celsius. Verkhoyansk in Russia, has recorded temperatures ranging from -68° Celsius to 32°Celsius. That is a huge range of temperatures to which living things have to **adapt**.

The trees of the forest

Northern forests do not have the variety of trees that forests in milder southern climates have. **Conifers** provide most of the **vegetation** in the boreal forest. These trees are well adapted to the extreme weather conditions of the boreal biome and its poor soils.

Black and white spruce, jack pine and balsam fir are typical trees of the northern forest. Black spruce tend to grow in areas that are wet and poorly drained. White spruce grow in better drained soils with more **nutrients**. In some parts of the northern forest there may be nothing but black spruce trees stretching far into the distance.

In the southern parts of the forest, deciduous trees such as poplars and birch grow among the conifers. The deciduous trees grow in places where the soils are richer and the weather conditions are not so harsh.

Tree adaptations

Coniferous trees do not have the broad, flat leaves of the deciduous trees in the milder south. Their leaves have adapted to northern life. Evergreen trees have thin, needle-like leaves that are covered with a protective, waxy coating that helps prevent water loss. As their name suggests, evergreen trees keep

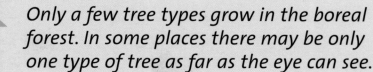
Only a few tree types grow in the boreal forest. In some places there may be only one type of tree as far as the eye can see.

their leaves all the year round. Unlike deciduous trees, they do not shed them in the autumn.

The shape of the taiga trees is also important. Rather than spreading out like deciduous trees, conifers are shaped like cones. This adaptation allows snow to fall more easily from their branches. This shape also allows strong winds to flow freely around the trees without damaging the branches. Birch trees, another kind of taiga tree, have supple trunks that bend easily under the weight of snow in the winter and then spring back undamaged when the spring thaw comes.

SPRING INTO ACTION

A tree's leaves capture sunlight to make food. Trees that shed their leaves in the autumn have to grow new ones before they can start making food again in the spring. Conifers, which keep their leaves all the year round, can begin producing food as soon as the weather warms up again. This is a useful adaptation in a climate where the growing season is short.

▼ *Boreal forest trees are shaped to shed snow much more easily than the trees of forests further south.*

Forest soil

The soil of the northern forests is waterlogged and has few nutrients. In the damp, cold conditions, plant and animal remains take a long time to decay, or break down. This means that nutrients are **recycled** very slowly.

Growth challenge

There is another reason for the poor condition of the forest soil. Trees produce poisons to discourage animals from eating them. When leaves are shed, these poisons enter the soil, slowing down the growth of the **microorganisms** that recycle plant and animal remains.

Some of the most northern areas of the forest have a layer of permafrost beneath the surface. This is soil that stays frozen throughout the year. Only the uppermost layer thaws in the summer. Permafrost trees are smaller, as they cannot put their roots down into the frozen soil. Larch trees are

At the northern edge of the forest, trees are small and widely spaced because the permafrost makes it difficult for them to take root.

Mushrooms are the above-ground parts of the fungi that are so important to the forest.

the most common. Further north, the forest blends into the low shrubs, grasses and mosses of the tundra.

Underground workers

Some of the most important living things in the forest are the fungi, which include moulds and mushrooms. They are essential recyclers, and help to decompose (or break down) forest debris, which releases nutrients and enriches the soil.

The relationship between underground fungi and tree roots is often a very close one. The fungi wrap themselves around the tree roots, protecting them from changes in temperature and providing them with nutrients from the soil. In return, the fungi take energy–rich sugar from the trees.

EVERGREEN ADVANTAGE

The evergreen trees of the northern forest do not shed their leaves every year. This helps them to grow in the taiga's nutrient-poor soils. As they do not need to make new leaves every year, they can make do with fewer nutrients than deciduous trees.

Forest plants

The taiga is dominated by trees, but a few other plants grow there as well. The undergrowth of the forest is a mixture of shrubs, flowering herbs, mosses and simple plants called lichens. Heather shrubs are common, as well as blueberries. Flowers such as wintergreen and creeping orchid grow among the shrubs. In drier areas of the forest, lichens may be the only plants growing on the forest floor.

 Sphagnum moss is a typical boreal plant, which grows abundantly in damp places.

Boreal bogs

Mosses grow abundantly in damp conditions. Low-lying bogs, called muskegs, are common throughout the boreal forest. Sphagnum moss forms a thick, spongy mat on the surface of the bog. Grasses and

shrubs grow on top of the mossy
mat, and spruce and larch trees grow
around the slightly drier edges of
the bog. Sphagnum moss helps to
maintain the damp conditions of the
bog. It acts like a sponge and holds
on to water – holding up to 40 times
its own weight! The solid layer of
moss also prevents water evaporating
from the bog underneath.

Insect-eaters

The boreal forest soil is not rich in
nutrients, so most plants have to
obtain their nutrients from another
source. Some of the most common
types of plants growing in the bogs
of the northern forest are those that
eat insects. These include pitcher
plants and sundews. Pitcher plants
have hollow stalks into which insects
fall and become trapped. Sundews
have sticky threads growing on
their leaves in which insects
become entangled.

Winter survival

During the winter months, when the forest is
covered with snow, most of the taiga plants die.
Only their underground parts survive, ready to
push back above the surface when the spring
thaw comes. Small shrubs are insulated from
the worst of the cold by blankets of snow.

Forest fires

A forest fire raging out of control is a frightening sight. A major fire can seem very destructive for the forest and the life it holds, but this isn't exactly the case. Careful study has shown that fires are a natural part of the cycles of growth in a forest.

Forest clearance

Fires are not always caused by careless campers – they can also be caused naturally by lightning strikes. Forest fires burn away the underbrush in the forest. This allows sunlight to reach the forest floor, where it encourages seeds to **germinate** and grow. Forest fires clear dead or diseased trees, along with the insects and other pests associated with those trees. Many animals are able to escape the fires and may colonize new territories as a result.

The ash left behind by a fire is rich in nutrients such as phosphorus, calcium and magnesium. These help to encourage new plant growth in the burned areas.

Aspen and birch are among the first trees to grow in the cleared soil. Later, spruce and fir trees join them.

As different plants colonize the newly-cleared ground, they provide a variety of food sources for a range of animals. Hares, deer and other plant-eaters soon arrive to feed on the new shoots. Other animals return to eat the seeds and berries of the new plants. Meat-eaters, such as the wolf, will eventually come to eat the plant-eaters.

Quaking aspen, balsam poplar and paper birch are all examples of trees that can spring up quickly from the forest sites that have been cleared by fire. These trees produce large numbers of lightweight seeds that are carried by the wind to the open ground.

New plants usually establish themselves quickly after a forest fire.

OUT OF THE ASHES

Some tree **species**, such as aspens and jack pines, need fires as part of their life cycles. The jack pine is a good example. It is often found growing in recently-burned areas. The cones of the jack pine will not germinate unless they are burned first.

Forest fires may not always be a bad thing, as they help to clear the ground for new growth.

Forest animals

Many types of animals have adapted to life in the boreal forest. The plant-eaters of the taiga have to survive on foods that are hard to digest. Some, such as the Siberian flying squirrel in Asia and the northern flying squirrel in North America, feed on the bark and cones of the conifers.

Moose are one of the largest plant-eaters in the northern forest. They prefer not to eat the tough needles and cones of the conifers. Instead, they feed on the more tender shrubs and herb plants. Caribou – large North American reindeer – eat lichens from the forest floor and digest conifer needles. This means that the two biggest plant-eaters have different diets, so they don't compete for food.

There are many large hunters in the boreal forest, including bears, wolves and lynx.

The lynx, a big cat, has unusually large feet, an adaptation that helps it walk across snow without sinking in. The lynx hunts birds, hares and rodents throughout the forests of North America, Europe and Asia. Furry hunters, such as the various members of the weasel family, are common in the northern forests. The plant-eaters on which they feed include squirrels, lemmings, voles and

 The flying squirrel glides through the forests of Scandinavia and Siberia.

Fishermen often catch northern pikes in the forest lakes.

snowshoe hares. As its name suggests, the snowshoe hare, like the lynx, has big feet for walking across the snow.

Forest fish

The boreal forest is dotted with lakes and crisscrossed by rivers and streams, so it isn't surprising that there are fish there as well. Many forest animals, including birds, moose, wolves, otters, beavers and bears, depend on the lakes for food, water and, in the case of the fish, a place to live. Bass and pike are typical lake fish.

Most of the life in the lakes is close to the shore. There the water is shallow and not so cold. Vegetation can take root, providing a food source for fish. Trees may also fall into the water, brought down by wind or beavers. The fallen trees provide food and

CRYSTAL CLEAR WATER

Northern lakes are very clear. This is because the water contains very few nutrients, so there is little food to support algae, bacteria and other microbes. The bottom of the lake is usually hard granite rock. Everything else was scraped away by glaciers during the last ice age.

shelter for fish. They are also good hiding sites for the fish that hunt other fish. As they decay, the trees act as a source of nutrients for water plants.

Surviving the winter

Any animal that lives in the boreal forest has to survive harsh winters. Many of the birds of the forest avoid the winter by **migrating** to warmer places when the weather becomes cold. Bears escape winter by **hibernating** in their dens until spring.

Some animals, including wolves and caribou, move into the forest for the winter, migrating from the colder tundra to the north. Insects, on the other hand, vanish from the forest during the winter. They survive as eggs or as hibernating **larvae**, ready to hatch or continue their life cycle when conditions improve.

Small **mammals** may hibernate for the winter. Hibernation allows animals to conserve energy when there is little food available. The woodchuck of North America, a type of ground squirrel, spends up to eight months of the year in an underground burrow about 150 centimetres below the surface. Other animals remain active throughout the year. Voles, for example, spend the winter tunnelling under the blanket of snow and feeding on plants.

▼ *The fierce wolverine has few enemies in the northern forest.*

Tiny shrews also stay active, relying on finding insect eggs and larvae to eat. The snow protects small animals from the cold and hides them from **predators**.

Black and brown bears in the coldest northern parts of the forest may spend from four to six months hibernating. Each bear digs out a den or crawls into a hollow log, rock cave or other sleeping area. In the spring, the bears slowly emerge from their dens. Females with newborn cubs are usually the last to appear.

Winter hunters

Weasels live throughout the boreal forests. They are small enough to live under the snow with the voles and shrews. Ermine, also called stoats, are slightly bigger forest hunters. They eat anything they can catch and they are fast enough to catch hares. Weasels and stoats both turn white in the winter. This adaptation makes them harder to spot by the animals they are hunting – and the animals that may be hunting them!

Martens, close relatives of the weasels and stoats, are common pine forest hunters. Like the stoat, the marten has a thick winter coat to protect it from the cold. The biggest member of this animal family is the ferocious wolverine. Although it is more of a **scavenger** than a hunter, the wolverine has powerful jaws that can cause serious harm to any animal that gets in its way.

The snowshoe hare is one of the most common forest animals. Its fur turns white in the winter.

Wolves

Wolves are adaptable hunters and can survive in many places where the climate is cold – as long as they can find enough to eat. The boreal forest, with its long, cold winters, short summers and wandering herds of deer and other **prey** animals, is ideal wolf territory.

Wolves are endangered today in most of North America, Europe and Asia, although there were once large numbers. They are staging a comeback in Alaska and Canada. The largest wolf population in the world now lives in the Siberian taiga of Russia.

The grey wolf is the world's largest wild canine, a close relative of the dog. Despite its name, the grey wolf isn't always grey. Its coat can be shades of grey, brown, white or even black. A full-grown adult stands about a metre tall at the shoulder and measures 1–1.5 metres in length from its nose to the tip of its long, bushy tail. A big wolf can weigh up to 79 kilograms, but 45–54 kilograms is more common. Male wolves are bigger than females.

The wolf has adapted in many ways to life in the northern forest. Its woolly fur provides excellent insulation against the biting wind, and it has long, water-repellent guard hairs which help to keep moisture

from reaching the wolf's skin. The claws of a wolf are well designed for gripping slippery surfaces, and its large paws can spread out to help prevent the wolf from sinking into the snow.

The tundra wolf is a type of grey wolf that lives in the forests of Scandinavia and Russia.

The wolf pack

Wolves are very social animals. They live in groups called packs. There can be as few as four or more than 30 wolves in a pack. A typical pack consists of an alpha male, the leader of the pack, and his mate, the alpha female. The rest of the pack is made up of their offspring, including young wolves from the previous year's litter and the current year's cubs. There may be some low-ranking adult wolves in the pack as well. Some lone wolves wander the forest on their own.

Wolf cubs are born around May or June in a den, which might be a hole in the ground or a space between rocks. During the eight weeks that the mother looks after her cubs, other members of the pack bring her food so she doesn't have to leave her cubs to hunt. The pack also guards the den against predators such as brown bears.

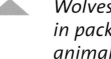
Wolves hunting together in packs can tackle bigger animals than a single wolf could on its own.

Grey hunters

Wolves catch and eat big animals such as moose, caribou and other forest deer. The pack tracks down a herd and picks out an old, sick or young animal to kill. By doing this wolves play a valuable role. Killing the sick and weak animals means that there is more food for the others, and the moose and caribou herds are healthier because of it. Wolves either wear down their prey in a long pursuit or make a sudden sprint to bring it down, depending on the circumstances. They also eat smaller animals such as squirrels and hares, when larger prey is scarce.

Moose on the loose

One of the most impressive animals of the northern forest is the moose. The moose is the largest member of the deer family. It lives in the boreal forests of North America and the taiga of Asia and Europe. Moose are most often seen near streams, lakes or in other wetland areas.

The moose looks like no other animal. It is a very large, stocky deer, with surprisingly long, slim legs. It has a large, horse-like head with a big nose. Males carry enormous antlers that can measure more than 1.8 metres across. A full-grown adult moose can weigh up to 495 kilograms and stand 1.8 metres tall.

A bull moose can have impressively large antlers.

Moose feast

Although the moose makes its home among the conifers of the boreal forest, it does not eat them. It feeds instead on the broad-leaved plants of the forest undergrowth. During the spring, summer and into the autumn, before the winter freeze comes, moose eat water plants. They can be seen browsing through marshes, in streams and along the shores of lakes, often wading out into fairly deep water. They look ungainly,

Water plants are a favourite part of the moose's diet.

but moose are very good, fast swimmers. During the winter, moose have to spend a lot of time finding enough to eat. Their great weight is useful when they are trampling down the snow to find bushes and tree saplings hidden underneath. Moose spend the winter feeding on twigs, bark and small tree saplings.

Moose behaviour

Moose can be seen at any time of day, but they are most active at night. Unlike many other types of deer that live in herds, the moose is a solitary animal. Apart from a female moose and her calves, moose are seldom seen together. A female moose is aggressive in the defence of her calves. Not even a wolf pack will tackle a full-grown, healthy moose.

The life of a moose

During the autumn, male moose, called bulls, roam the forest in search of females, called cows. The mating season lasts about a month and is called the moose rut. Both bulls and cows make sad-sounding, trumpeting calls to each other. Bulls often fight for the same cow, clashing their big antlers. After the mating season, males shed their antlers, and regrow them the following year.

Females give birth to their calves in the spring. There is usually one calf, sometimes two. Triplets are quite rare. Calves stay with their mother until the following spring. Then she chases them away so she can raise her next family. Moose can live up to 20 years, but 12 is considered old for a moose.

Bears in the woods

The bears of the northern forest are large, powerful animals. They have no enemies other than people. Brown bears live in Europe, northern Asia, Japan and North America. Large brown bears called grizzlies live in western parts of North America. The smaller black bear lives throughout the boreal forest and into the tundra of North America.

Colour confusion

Black bears are not always black, nor are brown bears always brown! Brown bears can vary in colour from light cream to dark brown or even black. The name grizzly bear comes from the long, white-tipped hairs that give the bear a grizzled appearance from a distance. Black bears are mostly black, but they can also be chocolate-coloured, creamy white or red-brown. There are even blond black bears!

What's that bear?

The brown bear ranges from 1.8–2.4 metres in length and is 1.2–1.4 metres tall at the shoulder. Black bears are usually smaller than brown bears, averaging 1.7 metres long and 0.75 metres tall. The brown bear

Fish is a nutritious meal for a hungry black bear.

Bears are solitary animals. Cubs stay with their mother for only their first two winters.

has a distinctive hump between its shoulders; the black bear has no hump.

The life of a bear

Both black and brown bears are solitary creatures. The only exceptions are female bears and their cubs. Bear cubs are born in a maternity den in January or February. There may be as many as five cubs in a litter, but the average is two. They stay with their mother until they are about a year and a half old.

Bear necessities

Bears have a varied diet. They eat grasses, plant bulbs and roots, nuts and berries. Brown bears eat big animals such as reindeer and moose, feast on salmon as they swim upriver to their spawning grounds, and snack on insects and

BIG BEARS

Bears vary a lot in size, depending on what there is to eat. Male brown bears can weigh between 135 and 390 kilograms. The biggest brown bears are the Kodiak bears of British Columbia and Alaska.

small **mammals** such as mice and squirrels. Black bears will also eat just about anything they can get their paws on, including insects, eggs, small mammals and other animals' leftovers.

Boreal bird life

There are several birds in the northern forest that have adapted to feed on the coniferous trees. Down on the forest floor, members of the grouse family, such as the spruce grouse of North America and the capercaillie of Europe, feed on conifer needles. Capercaillies can grow big on this diet. A male bird can weigh 8 kilograms!

Crossbills, a type of finch, are adapted to extract seeds from pine cones. Their beaks overlap at the tip, which allows the birds to cut through the scales of the pine cones to reach the seeds inside. The pine grosbeak also feeds on cones. It uses its heavy bill to smash open the cones.

Insect-eating birds, such as flycatchers and warblers, visit the forest only during the brief summer, when there is plenty for them to eat. Woodpeckers stay longer than other insect-eaters because they are able to reach

Crossbills are well adapted for extracting seeds from pine cones.

◄ *The boreal owl is common in the northern forest, although rarely seen. In Europe, it is known as Tengmalm's owl.*

the insect larvae that hide in tree bark. Ravens eat anything that's available and live in the forest all the year round.

Birds of prey

Birds hunt by day and night in the boreal forest. Daytime hunters include hawks and eagles. They hunt other birds flying above the treetops or snatch martens from the branches. The goshawk is an agile hunter in both North American and Eurasian forests. It hunts birds in the summer and squirrels in the winter.

Various owls patrol the night-time forest. They feed largely on rodents, which, like the owls, are active at night. Owls have keen eyesight, which allows them to spot the slightest movement, even in the heart of a forest at night. They also have fantastically good hearing and can pinpoint the direction of a sound with great accuracy. The great grey owl is a large owl that lives deep in the northern forest. It blends in so well with the background that it is rarely seen.

Threats to the forest

The boreal forest may seem a remote wilderness, far from human influence, but even there, the effects of human activities are keenly felt.

Logging

Forestry has taken a heavy toll on the northern forest. In Scandinavia, almost all the wild boreal forest has vanished. It has been replaced by managed tree farms. The forests of Siberia and North America are still mostly intact, but the pressure on them is increasing as foresters move into new areas to take wood for papermaking.

Almost all the **logging** in the boreal forest involves clearcutting – taking in heavy machinery and stripping whole areas of their trees. The damage this causes to the forest is considerable, not just through removing the trees, but also in creating logging roads to move the **timber** out. In the cold conditions of the boreal forest, trees take longer to grow back than they do in the warmer forests further south, so a forest may not recover from logging damage for many years – if at all.

Hydroelectric hazards

Hydroelectric dams have been built in the boreal forest. These dams can completely alter the forest landscape, flooding large areas of the forest and changing the paths of streams and rivers. Hydroelectric dams provide people with a relatively clean

The demand for timber products is one of the biggest threats to the northern forest.

source of energy, but they can also harm the area's wildlife by destroying their habitats forever.

Other threats

Other threats to the forest come from drilling oil wells and digging mines. Constructing roads into the forest to serve these industries also causes a great deal of damage to the environment.

What can be done?

During the last century, paper consumption (usage) increased 20 times. Meeting the demand for paper is one of the major forces which drives loggers into the boreal forest. One important thing that everyone can do to help save the forest is to use fewer paper and wood products. Try to recycle

 Forest visitors must take care to do as little damage as possible to this fragile biome.

newspapers, magazines and cardboard whenever possible.

The boreal forest is such a special place that people naturally want to visit it. However, delicate ground plants are threatened by backpackers and other visitors trampling on them. As more people go into the forest, the likelihood of an accidental forest fire increases. People should treat the northern forest with the respect it deserves. If everyone plays their part in caring for the forest, the green crown around the head of the world will continue to grow for generations to come.

Glossary

adapt To become suited to life in a particular environment.

Arctic Circle An imaginary line around the north polar regions.

biomes Large areas of the environment with distinctive climates and plant types; examples include forests, mountains and deserts.

climate The general weather conditions in a particular area.

conifers Evergreen trees. Conifers bear cones and often have needle-like leaves.

deciduous Having leaves that fall off at the end of one growing season and regrow at the start of the next one.

evaporate To change from a liquid into a vapour (or gas) without boiling. Puddles of rainwater disappear as they evaporate in sunshine.

forestry The science of looking after and maintaining forests.

germinate To start to grow. When a seed grows and produces its first root and leaves, it has germinated.

glaciers Slow-moving rivers of ice that move down from the snowfields at the tops of mountains.

habitat The place where a living thing makes its home; the environment that it is adapted to survive in.

hibernating Being in a state of hibernation. This is how some animals survive long, cold winters. Their breathing and heart rate slows, their body temperature drops, and they fall into a sleep-like state that lasts until conditions improve.

hydroelectric To do with electricity generated by running water.

ice age A period in Earth's history when the average temperature dropped and glaciers spread north and south from the polar regions. The last major ice age ended about 10,000 years ago.

larvae (singular form: larva) The stage between hatching from an egg and adulthood in animals whose young look very different from the adults, such as insects.

logging Cutting down large areas of forest to use the wood.

mammals Animals that are warm-blooded and usually have hair on their skin, including humans and moose. Female mammals produce milk to feed their young.

microorganisms Living things that are so small they can be seen only by using a microscope.

migrating Moving from one place to another in search of better living conditions.

nutrients Another word for food; all the things needed for a balanced diet to provide energy and raw materials for the growth and maintenance of the organism.

permafrost A layer of soil that is permanently frozen.

predators Animals that catch and eat other animals for their food.

prey Animals that are caught and eaten by predators.

recycled Made available to use again.

scavenger An animal that feeds on the dead remains of other animals.

species A group of living things with the same general appearance and behaviour, which can breed together to produce fertile offspring.

taiga The Russian name for the northern boreal forest that lies to the south of the tundra.

timber Wood that is used for building.

tundra A region of the cold north where there is a layer of permanently frozen earth beneath the topsoil, few trees can grow and the vegetation is mainly grasses and mosses.

vegetation The plant life in an area.

Index